Rocks and Sticks

by John Wood

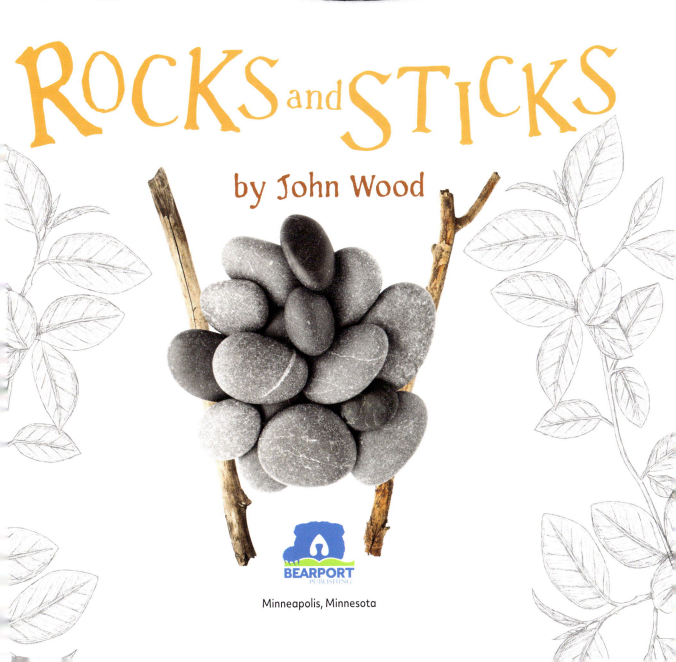

BEARPORT
PUBLISHING

Minneapolis, Minnesota

Credits:
Front Cover — Nik Merkulov, Natalia van D, Julia Sudnitskaya, Liuba Bilyk, 2&3 — Creative Lab, 4&5 — Monkey Business Images, Tatiana Gordievskaia, 6&7 — Denis Kuvaev, ziggy_mars, 8&9 — Chalabala, Taigi, 10&11 — Emilio Amato, Nordic Studio, 12&13 — Bilanol, Trofimov Denis, 14&15 —Gillian Pullinger, Elmar Langle, 16&17 — JGA, Rejean Bedard, 18&19 — FatCamera, Sparkling Moments Photography, 20&21 — CarpathianPrince, theFinnch, Mr.Winter, 22&23 — dmphoto, shutting.
Images are courtesy of Shutterstock.com. With thanks to Getty Images, Thinkstock Photo, and iStockphoto.

Library of Congress Cataloging-in-Publication Data is available at www.loc.gov or upon request from the publisher.

ISBN: 978-1-63691-463-3 (hardcover)
ISBN: 978-1-63691-470-1 (paperback)
ISBN: 978-1-63691-477-0 (ebook)

© 2022 Booklife Publishing
This edition is published by arrangement with Booklife Publishing.

North American adaptations © 2022 Bearport Publishing Company. All rights reserved. No part of this publication may be reproduced in whole or in part, stored in any retrieval system, or transmitted in any form or by any means, electronic, mechanical, photocopying, recording, or otherwise, without written permission from the publisher.

For more information, write to Bearport Publishing, 5357 Penn Avenue South, Minneapolis, MN 55419. Printed in the United States of America.

CONTENTS

Welcome to the Forest **4**
Taking Care of Nature. **6**
Super Sticks. **8**
Rock On! **10**
Biggest and Smallest. **12**
Bugs and Plants **14**
Home Builders. **16**
Walking with Sticks **18**
Get Making! **20**
Time to Think. **22**
Glossary **24**
Index **24**

Welcome to the Forest

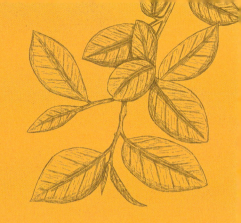

Welcome to forest school.
Let's explore, play, and create!

Get ready for forest fun!

What do you want to learn about the forest?

We can learn so much from the world around us. Step outside into a great big classroom full of trees, animals, sticks, and rocks.

5

Taking Care of Nature

Any time we go into **nature**, we must take care of it. We should leave the forest as we found it.

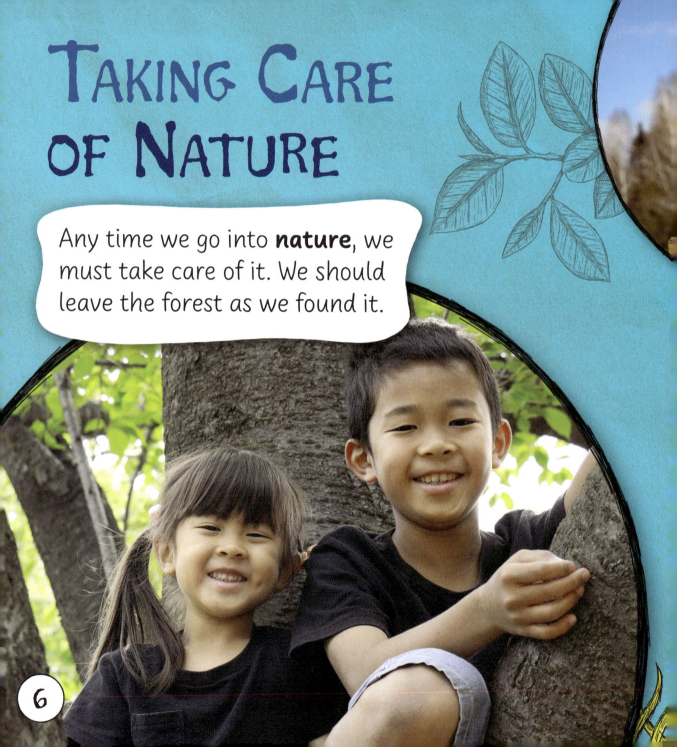

6

Super Sticks

The forest has sticks and rocks all over the ground. Let's look at the sticks first! Sticks are pieces of wood that have fallen off trees or bushes.

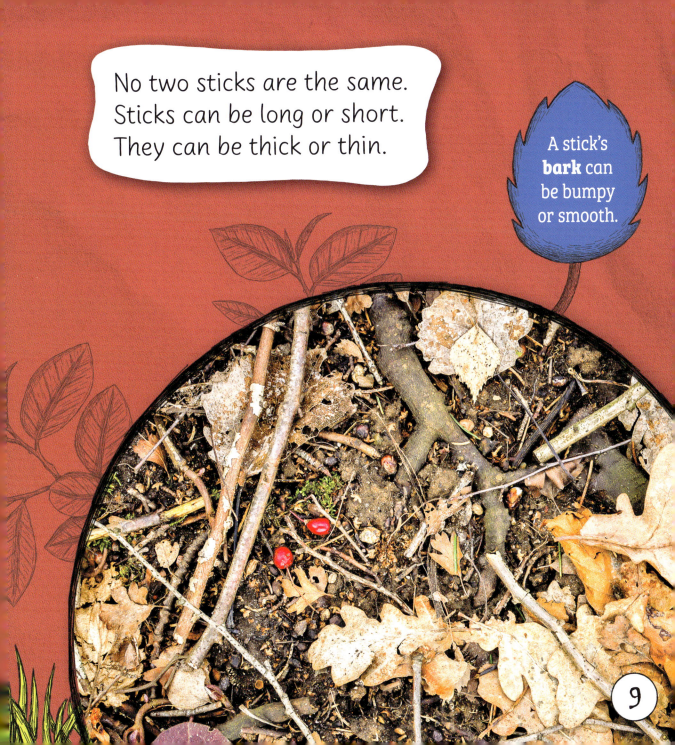

No two sticks are the same. Sticks can be long or short. They can be thick or thin.

A stick's **bark** can be bumpy or smooth.

Rock On!

Rocks often form underground. Then, they are pushed up to the **surface**. This takes a very long time.

Every rock is different. Some are round and smooth. Others have sharp edges. Rocks can be flat or bumpy.

Remember to be careful with rocks and sticks. Never throw them.

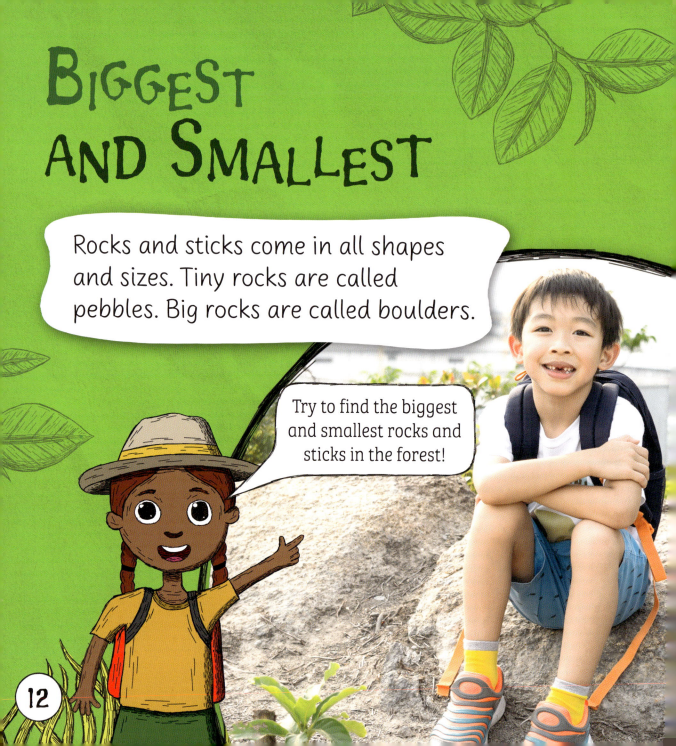

Small sticks might easily break. But bigger sticks are stronger!

Little sticks are called twigs. Big fallen branches are sticks, too.

13

Bugs and Plants

Rocks and sticks are helpful to other parts of the forest. Many bugs live under rocks or sticks.

Some bugs eat the wood from sticks.

After sticks fall off trees, they are no longer alive.

Sticks on the ground slowly break down. They become **soil**. The soil helps plants grow.

Home Builders

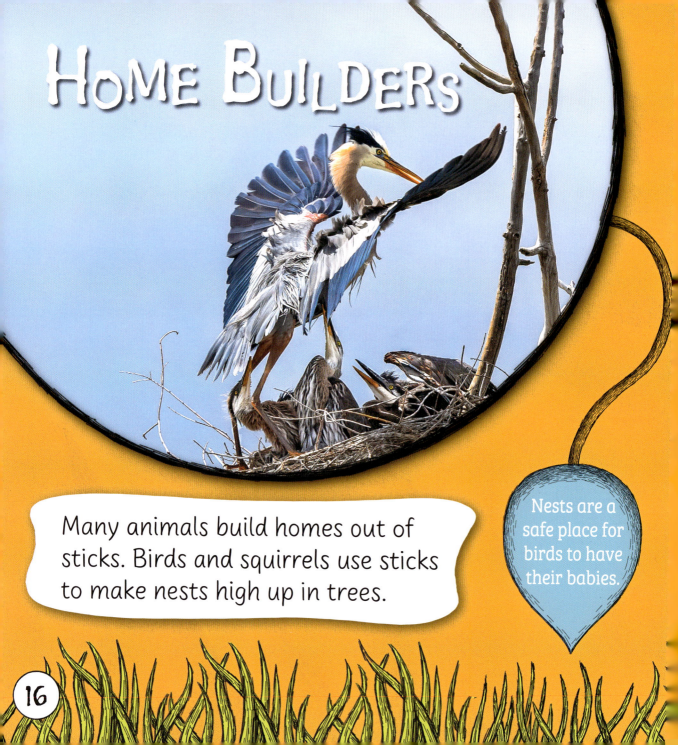

Many animals build homes out of sticks. Birds and squirrels use sticks to make nests high up in trees.

Nests are a safe place for birds to have their babies.

Other animals use sticks to build homes on the ground. Beavers and woodrats do this.

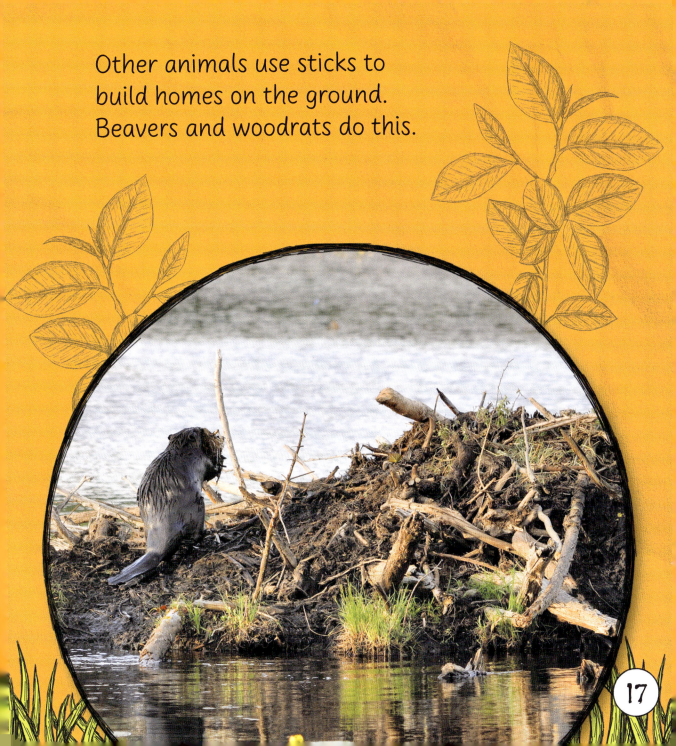

Walking with Sticks

Sticks are useful for people, too! Some people use sticks to help them walk on forest trails.

Remember to take your walking stick from the ground rather than a tree.

Can you find the perfect walking stick? Look for one that is long and straight. It should be strong.

19

Get Making!

Sticks and rocks can make great art **materials**. Have they sparked your **creativity**?

Did you know that rocks often change color when they're wet?

Gather some rocks and place them in a bowl. Add water and see them change colors. It's art!

You can stack rocks to make cool shapes.

How tall can you make your stack of rocks?

21

What did you learn about rocks and sticks? And how did learning about nature make you feel?

What do you want to explore next time at forest school?

GLOSSARY

bark a tree's outer covering

creativity the ability to imagine, make new things, or think new thoughts

litter things that have been thrown on the ground

materials things that can be used to make something else

nature the world and everything in it that is not made by people

soil dirt that plants grow in

surface the top of something, such as the top of the ground

INDEX

animals 5, 7, 16–17
boulders 12
branches 13
bugs 14
pebbles 12
plants 7, 14–15
soil 15
trees 5, 8, 15–16, 18
twigs 13